Pebble®

Polar Animals

Snowy Owls

by Helen Frost

Consulting Editor: Gail Saunders-Smith, PhD

Consultant: Brian M. Barnes, Director
Institute of Arctic Biology
University of Alaska, Fairbanks

Capstone
press®

Mankato, Minnesota

Pebble Books are published by Capstone Press,
151 Good Counsel Drive, P.O. Box 669, Mankato, Minnesota 56002.
www.capstonepress.com

Library of Congress Cataloging-in-Publication Data
Frost, Helen, 1949–
    Snowy owls / by Helen Frost.
    p. cm.—(Pebble books. Polar animals)
    Summary: "Simple text and photographs present snowy owls, where they live,
and what they do"—Provided by publisher.
    Includes bibliographical references (p. 23) and index.
    ISBN 978-0-7368-4246-4 (hardcover)
    ISBN 978-1-4296-4228-6 (saddle-stitch)
    1. Snowy owl—Juvenile literature. I. Title. II. Series.
QL696.S83F726 2007
598.9'7—dc22   2004026899

Note to Parents and Teachers

The Polar Animals set supports national science standards related
to life science. This book describes and illustrates snowy owls.
The images support early readers in understanding the text. The
repetition of words and phrases helps early readers learn new
words. This book also introduces early readers to subject-specific
vocabulary words, which are defined in the Glossary section. Early
readers may need assistance to read some words and to use the
Table of Contents, Glossary, Read More, Internet Sites, and Index
sections of the book.

Table of Contents

What Are Snowy Owls?

Snowy owls are
large white birds.
Some snowy owls have
dark spots.

areas where snowy owls live

Where Snowy Owls Live

Snowy owls live
on the tundra
in the far north.
The tundra is a cold place
without trees.

Body Parts

Feathers cover snowy owls.
They even have feathers
on their legs and feet.
The feathers keep
them warm.

Snowy owls have
strong wings.
They soar over the tundra
to look for prey.

Snowy owls have
yellow eyes.
They can see well.
They watch for prey
moving on the tundra.

Snowy owls have
sharp claws.
They stretch out
their claws to catch prey.

What Snowy Owls Do

Snowy owls catch and eat birds, fish, and other small animals.

Snowy owls nest
in shallow holes
in the ground.
Females stay
with their young.

Snowy owls perch
on rocks to rest.

Glossary

bird—a warm-blooded animal with two legs, wings, feathers, and a beak

claw—a hard curved nail on the foot of a bird or other animal

feather—one of the light fluffy parts that cover a bird's body

nest—to find a place to lay eggs and bring up young

perch—to stand on the edge of something; snowy owls perch on rocks on the tundra to rest and to look around for prey.

prey—an animal that is hunted by another animal for food

shallow—not deep

tundra—a flat, cold area without trees; the ground stays frozen in the tundra for most of the year.

Read More

Glassman, Jackie. *Amazing Arctic Animals.* All Aboard Science Reader. New York: Grosset & Dunlap, 2002.

Townsend, Emily Rose. *Owls.* Pebble Books: Woodland Animals. Mankato, Minn.: Capstone Press, 2004.

Internet Sites

FactHound offers a safe, fun way to find Internet sites related to this book. All of the sites on FactHound have been researched by our staff.

Here's how:

1. Visit *www.facthound.com*
2. Choose your grade level.
3. Type in this book ID **0736842462** for age-appropriate sites. You may also browse subjects by clicking on letters, or by clicking on pictures and words.
4. Click on the **Fetch It** button.

FactHound will fetch the best sites for you!

23

Index

Word Count: 124
Grade: 1
Early-Intervention Level: 14

Editorial Credits

Martha E. H. Rustad, editor; Patrick D. Dentinger, designer; Wanda Winch, photo
researcher; Scott Thoms, photo editor

Photo Credits

Bruce Coleman Inc./Dennis Fast–Visual & Written, 10; Joe McDonald, 8
Corbis/Daniel J. Cox, 18; Wolfgang Kaehler, 6
David Louis Flores, 14
Minden Pictures/Gerry Ellis, cover; Michio Hoshino, 16; Tim Fitzharris, 12
Peter Arnold Inc./C. Allan Morgan, 20
Photodisc/Alan and Sandy Carey, 1
Visuals Unlimited/Bill Banaszewski, 4